Let This Mind

Biblical Principles from the Greatest Entrepreneur of All

Lawron Ballard

Let This Mind
Print ISBN: 979-8-218-21143-1

www.lawronballard.com
Editorial Work: Megan Ryan
Design: Andrew Carroll - 42 Design Co. • https://42design.co

Table of contents

Section 2: The Gospel Business Marketplace Case Studies

Introduction

You shouldn't read this book. I know that's not what you expected me to say. That goes contrary to what every author says about their writing, but not me. Why? Because I mean it.

If your goal is to maintain the status quo...
and to continue living the way you have been...
...then you shouldn't go a step further.

This book is for the few brave ones who are looking to be stretched, challenged, shifted, encouraged, and motivated.

Entrepreneurship is as much a mindset game as it is strategies and tactics, but you wouldn't know it from the outside looking in. Instead, what we see is the Instagram and YouTube highlights, but we have no idea the cost. Because of this, a poor, unsuspecting dreamer goes into the world attempting to effect change, and three months, six months, or one year later, they go back to their 9 to 5 with their tails between their legs.

It's not their fault. They simply didn't know what they didn't know.

James 1 tells us that trials are always for our development, but somehow, we miss this. Society has conditioned us to strive to get things right. Mistakes show lack of competency. Struggling means you're not supposed to do it. But if you don't change your perspective, you can never get ahead.

I wish someone had told me this.

I think about all the heartache and self-pity I allowed myself to wallow in because I simply didn't understand that business is more than applying information. It's about transformation.

While I don't believe everyone is called to be an entrepreneur, I do believe that for those who are called, it's an instrument for character development in the hand of the Master.

As I look back at the transformation that has happened in my life in my pursuit of creating a profitable business, I can't help but marvel.

God is so gracious, loving, and wise. He knows the best tools to equip and strengthen us to reach His ultimate goal of cultivating in us the mind of Christ.

Imagine what the world would be like if we had a league of profitable, purpose-driven entrepreneurs who let the mind of Christ become theirs.

What schools would be started?
What non-profits would be created?
How many jobs would be added?

How much faster could the gospel be spread in order to hasten the coming of our Lord?

The possibilities are endless, but we need to surrender.

I wrote this book with the intention of sparking as many people to action as possible.

I want you to see that the calling to entrepreneurship comes with an infinite amount of promises to help you meet the demands.

I want this book to be a source of inspiration and encouragement to keep pushing when times get tough.

This is the book that I wish I had when I was at my lowest.

The principles outlined in this book are not hard, but it will require you to be honest with yourself. To see where you're lacking and ask God to transform you into who you need to be in order to achieve your dreams.

This book was a divine assignment, and I pray that my love for God, for business, and for your purpose shines through each page.

Lawron Ballard
2021

About This Book

This book is designed to be inspirational and instructional, and it is divided into two sections. Section One includes a combination of personal stories from my time as a restaurant owner, biblical insights, and a framework I call the Christ Mind Method. Section Two is a series of real-world examples written in a case study format and looks at how Christ would address the issues.

Personal Stories

From January 2019 until March 2020, I was a part owner of a small restaurant in southeastern Pennsylvania. While I had attempted entrepreneurship prior to opening the restaurant, that was my first real attempt at running a business. Interwoven between the teaching elements of the book, you will find journal-style entries that document the highs and lows of that experience. Please note that they not chronological, but they are organized in a way to support the framework.

Biblical Insights

As a Christian, I believe that the Bible is the ultimate source of truth and guidance for all aspects of life. In the book, I will share some of the biblical insights that I have gleaned over the years as a Bible student and a business owner.

The Framework

In the book, I discuss what it takes to go from being the Sinking CEO to the Liberated Leader. The Sinking CEO, who we will define later in the book, is struggling with their faith and managing their business and their relationships, and generally feels out of control. The Liberated Leader, on the other hand, is empowered to do and be more. They look at the challenges they face in business from a position of hopefulness and have the clarity of mind to make the best decisions possible. It is my mission to help thousands of entrepreneurs to make that transition from chaos to order in their business and in their lives using a process I call the Christ Mind Method.

The Christ Mind Method includes four elements: Self-Discovery, Biblical Framing, Thought Anatomy, and the R.E.W.I.R.E. Toolkit. While seemingly insignificant by themselves, they all come together perfectly to help faith-based entrepreneurs become all God has called them to be.

The Christ Mind Method teaches you the following:

1. **Self-Discovery**: This is all about understanding what makes you you. It's about understanding your strengths, weaknesses, and how they impact your business.
2. **Biblical Framing**: This is the concept of allowing Scripture to be how we make decisions and interpret the marketplace and challenges you face.
3. **Thought Anatomy**: This element is all about understanding where thoughts come from and why we as believers need to learn how to master the real estate between our ears.
4. **R.E.W.I.R.E. Toolkit**: This is where you will learn some practical skills to replace any negative thoughts and behaviors that you've cultivated as an entrepreneur with positive and God-honoring practices.

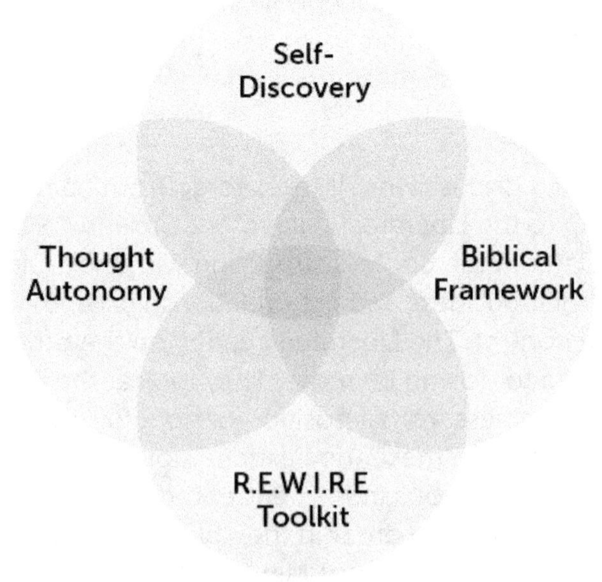

You may be wondering why you need these four elements. Let me give you an example. You're an entrepreneur and you know that you do good work, but when it's time to deliver your services to your clients, you get immense anxiety. You go through the process of looking at your situation through biblical framing. You know that your thoughts of inadequacy aren't God's thoughts towards you, and you have the toolkit that can help you work through these thoughts and change them, but if you do, you have no idea how to measure if there's been a change.

Self-discovery would help you see that your thoughts of inadequacy and self-doubt resulted in procrastination and time management issues. By having this clarity, you can more specifically address areas of weakness from the root to the fruit.

We'll explore all these elements in more detail later in the book.

Case Studies

Finally, after we've gone through the framework, the last section of the book is a series of case studies. These case studies are based on common problems I have seen or experienced in the entrepreneurial space. They are laid out in a problem-solution format, and they look at Jesus's earthly ministry in order to learn how He would address them. These case studies are the tip of the iceberg and should be used as a model to look at challenges that may arise in your own business.

August 31, 2021

I never thought I'd write a book. Okay, maybe I thought about it, but I didn't take it seriously. Nevertheless, this whole year, I've been feeling this nagging to write. About what? I wasn't sure. That didn't stop the thoughts from coming. Today was different, though. It wasn't a "nagging" anymore, but a deep conviction that the transformation I've undergone over the last couple years wasn't solely for me.

A lot has changed since the business closed, and while I don't have it all figured out, I know for sure that what I've learned in this short amount of time is supposed to be shared with the world.

The craziest part of this whole book thing is not the writing itself, but how do I articulate the truths that I've discovered in a meaningful way? I have no idea, but I'm trusting the Giver of the assignment. If He has tasked me, then I must have some untapped potential that He's trying to draw out.

Here goes nothing.

-L

The Gospel Business

Every good book starts with a story, and this one is no different. This is the story of CJ, a young entrepreneur who was bold, daring, innovative, insightful, and caring, but also, unlike so many of us, he knew that he only had a few short years to live.

You see, for years, CJ wanted to be a part of the business his father had started called "Cure." Cure's mission was to find the remedy for a life-threatening disease that, in many cases, went undetected. For years, CJ had watched as different treatments were tested, but he knew that even though they were helpful, they weren't the answer. Finally, the Cure formula was complete, and it was just a little while longer before it would be available to the public.

Being the only child, CJ felt an unspeakable burden for the business. He knew what his father was trying to build, and it was up to him to make it happen. Despite his eagerness, the young man waited because he knew that when the time was right, his father would tell him. Then came his thirtieth birthday. It was finally time, and he was ready. As soon as he got the word, CJ purposed in his heart to spend his remaining years telling as many people as he could about Cure and making his father proud.

Straightaway, CJ got to work. He started to build relationships with people in his community. He served whoever he could, unbothered by his lack of time or resources. As he met people, he was drawn to them with a deep compassion. Desiring to give them the best that he had to offer, he looked for ways to make their lives better by knowing him.

As he worked, CJ kept his eyes open for the people best suited to move the business forward after he was gone. One might think that the ideal successor would be the one who is the most educated, the most well-connected, the most well-informed, someone who looked great on paper. Except CJ viewed people differently. He was more concerned with the heart of his team. He knew that if he found people with a teachable spirit, he could help them reach their highest potential. He looked for that spark in their eye that nobody else seemed to notice. He knew what it was like to be overlooked, and he made it a point for no one to feel that way under his care.

The business started to pick up steam. CJ and his team went from casual meetings with people to planning live lectures and hosting food drives and health fairs. The more they worked and served, the more people began to take notice. Everyone was curious about how this unassuming man, who had no connections and seemingly no resources, was able to do so much with such a motley crew.

His team liked the attention. They had never been at the forefront of the media and the topic of conversation like they were as they went from town to town, city to city, building up this company. But CJ wasn't fazed. He knew that there was an limit on the amount of time he could spend building this business. He needed everyone to know about Cure. And he needed his team to understand that what they were trying to bring to the market was bigger than the freebies. The product Cure had would change lives forever. So even if they didn't see the vision, he stayed laser focused.

When his team didn't really understand what they were building, CJ knew. They lost sight of the mission; CJ didn't. Regardless of the disappointments or their lack of dedication at times, he tried to train them and coach them. He took them on retreats. He privately coached them and cultivated their ability to be salesmen, but also leaders. They were the future generation of the company.

In the moments when CJ felt alone or misunderstood, he would call his father and they would talk. It was in those conversations that he knew he was doing exactly what he was supposed to be doing.

And so, day by day, step by step, getting closer and closer to the end of his life, he persevered; he served people and used opportunities to bring value to the marketplace. A lot of people would sell the things that he was giving for free. But he knew that if he could get them in—that if he could get them to know, like, and trust him—ultimately, they would be customers and purchase the real product that he was trying to sell.

It didn't matter if it meant more time; it didn't matter if it meant more energy; it didn't matter if it meant more resources. It was necessary. He deemed it a worthy investment to invest in people, so that they would have the opportunity to get close enough to him or to a member of his team and actually purchase the product.

It's kind of sad to hear about an entrepreneur so promising whose life was cut short. But, fortunately for us, this is not just any entrepreneur, for CJ is Christ Jesus. And that team that He built out was made up of the apostles that built the early church and carried on the legacy of our Lord and Savior. But whenever we hear the gospel, we never think about it as an endeavor, as an entrepreneurial endeavor, as a business. But Christ was always about His Father's business.

And so it is through this lens that we look at Philippians 2:5, which tells us, "Let this mind be in you, which was also in Christ Jesus." It's through this lens we can consider that verse to not just be speaking about the religious aspects of our life and our human experience, but we can look at it as a way to view business. We can look at Christ as a master entrepreneur, as a mogul, as a maven. And if we want to learn how to succeed in business, we can begin by looking at how Christ ran His.

But for the longest time, I really didn't understand this. I've always wanted to be an entrepreneur. I had dreams about it as a teenager. After graduating from college, I tried little things here and there. I got my first LLC at the age of twenty-three. But I had no idea what I was doing.

Fast forward to age thirty, when I finally had my first "real business." I opened a restaurant. And I did not realize how much my mind needed to change. But I believe that every single time we hit a snag, every time there is a failure, it is an opportunity for us to learn. It's an opportunity for us to view our circumstances and situations as chances for us to grow, to mature, to expand, to see the weak parts in our character and abilities and to adapt.

And so, in this book, we will look at the challenges of life. We'll consider how our minds need to change so that we can be successful in the marketplace. But then I want to add an additional caveat: What does that mean for us as believers? Is our aim just to make money? Is our aim just to have a seven- or eight-figure business? Or is there something deeper? Are we to look at our business the same way that Christ looked at His? Are we to see our good works as an opportunity to build, know, like, and trust? If so, is it just so someone will buy another product from us, or is it perhaps an opportunity for us to be affiliates of the kingdom?

I'm going to transition, as we go through our journey together, between the language of the gospel and the language of business. I want you to start to see that they're not different. They're the same. And our success in spirituality, our success in our Christian walk, and the foundations that we need to be successful unto salvation are the same that we need to be successful in business.

The very idea that the Bible can even be a tool for business is so countercultural. When was the last time you heard a business owner checking her marketing plan or customer service policies against what the Bible says? It's like we've completely separated our faith from our everyday lives. However, when we look at the business of Christ, we see that everything He did was actuated by God's Word. Similarly, as Christ followers, we should train ourselves to see the practicality of the Bible. It's from this framework, this foundation, this vantage point that we must look at everything because without a foundation, we are surely on sinking sand.

January 25, 2020

This place is sinking ... FAST. And I'm sinking right along with it. Every direction I go in seems to dead end at a closed door. I've tried everything from promotions and ads to adding more money into the business and even renegotiating contracts all in the hopes of turning this money pit around, but I can't seem to catch a break.

Oh, let's not even discuss the exhaustion. I am literally exhausted in every way possible—physically, emotionally, spiritually.

First it was the weekly commuting between NY and Philly trying to maintain a full-time job and a fledgling business. I was so busy trying to please everyone that I ended up overextending myself, and everyone involved suffered.

Then it's the bills. We always need something at the restaurant. Ingredients, supplies, bandages, maintenance. I've got contractors calling and emailing me all the time trying to get the money we owe them. Those are the types of calls and emails that ruin your day. I've never had this level of anxiety about money until now. We're barely making enough money to cover our costs, and it breaks my heart to tell the team. I've been trying to make up the difference with the money from my job, but that fell through back in November when I was forced to leave.

Don't mention how this has placed me in a weird space in terms of my faith. I thought that this is what God wanted, so why isn't it working? I'm to the point now where I just want this to end. I want to stop the bleeding and move on from this.

I feel like I'm suffocating. The stress of it all has taken a toll on my relationships, as well.

I got some contract work to make ends meet. It'll help bring in some cash to keep things going and keep my mind occupied by something other than this. It may not be my dream, but at least it makes sense.

-L

Section 1:
Christ Mind Method

The Two Minds

The principle of opposites finds its origins in the wisdom of God. In the beginning, God separated the darkness and the light. Day by day, the pattern continues making its presence known in everything from the heavens to human beings.

The very essence of our human experience takes its rhythmic cues from creation. Husband and wife. Parent and child. Inhale and exhale. Asleep and awake. Whether it's us in relation to other people or the processes of the body systems, there's always an equal and opposite side.

The realm of business is no different. I have found—maybe or maybe not from personal experience—that there are only two types of entrepreneurs: the Sinking CEO and the Liberated Leader.

The difference between the two isn't money, success, or influence. It isn't experience or industry. The only difference is perspective. The Liberated Leader chooses the lens of optimism and abundance as her worldview. The Sinking CEO chooses pessimism and lack.

We can be either or but never both. It is a choice to look beyond circumstance, and you are the only one who can make it.

Take the Sinking CEO. She is completely stuck.

She's tired. Overworked. Discouraged by the circumstances.

The challenges of business cause her to second guess her abilities. She loves to be in control, but because it feels like everything is out of control, she panics. She becomes overly burdened by the financial responsibilities of her current situation. Mentally, she is spread too thin and can't think beyond making ends meet.

She needs help, but her pride restrains her. Since she is unable to think clearly, her actions begin to strain the relationships that mean the most. Unsatisfied and unhappy, she finds it hard to enjoy her loved ones.

The Sinking CEO tries to seek help outside of herself, and even though she goes to church every week, it seems like she can't get a breakthrough. Her faith wavers. Doubt and depression follow suit. What was meant to be a blessing has turned into a curse.

She has become so consumed by what's going wrong that she becomes blind to the opportunities available to her even in the midst of chaos.

The Liberated Leader, on the other hand, is confident.

She stands firm in her faith and in the liberty with which Christ has set her free, knowing that her God will supply all her needs.

Even when things aren't their best, this type of entrepreneur looks for the lesson. She searches for the providence of God. She stands, like Christ, unshaken in the face of adversity. The confidence she has in God's Word and her God-given ability gives her courage to persevere. Because she views the world from an empowered vantage point, she sees opportunity in every storm.

How did the Liberated Leader become so optimistic? Was she born that way or is there something deeper?

When we think about Christ and we ask for the mind of Christ, we're not just asking to have victory over the temptations in our lives. We're asking to have victory in every aspect of the human experience. Imagine what the mind of Christ would do for you as a leader and for your team. Imagine how having the mind of Christ would impact and improve the level of service that you provide to your customers and clients. Think about what it means to strategize like Christ and how that would impact your marketing. There is literally nothing that would be left undone or be poorly executed if we would just surrender to this idea that the mind of Christ is a strategic mind.

By adopting the mind of Christ, we become the Liberated Leader.

Thinking about the amount that He was able to accomplish in three and a half years of ministry still amazes me. Regardless of how people received Him, how the disciples supported Him, or whether people accepted Him, Jesus remained unmoved by the waves of life. His peace was the result of the freedom and joy found in abiding in the Father's love.

In addition to His example of how to live a sanctified life, Christ also is the perfect case study for operational excellence and business development. Even more amazing is that the tactics He employed are four simple elements that I call the Christ Mind Method. Although simple, they made Jesus the most transformational leader the world has ever seen.

And these same four elements are the key to moving any entrepreneur away from being the Sinking CEO and propelling them to become the Liberated Leader.

April 12, 2019

I got my business cards today.

Name: *Lawron.* Title: *Owner.*

I stopped by the print shop to pick them up, and as I sat in the car and stared at them, I started to get anxious. Not in a bad way, but in a "hurry up already" kind of way.

This is what I've always wanted—to have something to call my own—and now it's finally happening.

Earlier today, we had a presentation at the local investors conference. We, along with other local business owners, came together to discuss the opportunities available in the community to really get in on the revitalization. It was exhilarating to be in the room with these types of people.

In addition to the networking and presentations, we had our first official debut as an up-and-coming restaurant.

Tony did almost all the shopping and preparation himself. He's really excited about what we have the potential to do. I appreciate him immensely. If it wasn't for him, we wouldn't be able to do half of what we've done.

We were really well received by the attendees, and I'm looking forward to sharing more of what we have to offer.

The road thus far hasn't been completely smooth, though. My dad and I had another investor end up pulling out right around the time we got the lease. It was a little discouraging, but we're going to continue to move forward.

Even with the setback, I'm anxious to realize this dream, to see the doors open and to finally be able to call myself a business owner. I wish I knew when we'll finally be open. There's just so much that needs to be done before that can happen.

I've been praying about it, but I'm like, "Lord, what's the holdup??" Maybe there's a lesson in the waiting.

I don't know. I haven't figured that part out yet.

-L

Element #1: Biblical Framing

Perception is everything. How we perceive life, ourselves, and others determines how we respond. This is good when our perceptions result in positive responses. The problem comes in when our perception causes us to respond in such a way that it damages our relationships and tarnishes our witness.

For the Christian, the Bible should be the lens we look through. Through it, the world and all the circumstances in it are properly understood and reacted to. Nevertheless, it seems like our Christianity dissipates as we leave the church steps and enter the marketplace.

How is it possible to be really, really good at spirituality in the pew but fall short in the boardroom? Just think about Solomon. This man had the most successful kingdom in all of Israel's history and wrote the book of Proverbs. In it are timeless principles related to team building, workmanship and integrity, relationship building, the economy, and more.

The book *Education* says this in reference to Solomon's instruction: "There is no branch of legitimate business for which the Bible does not afford an essential preparation. Its principles of diligence, honesty, thrift, temperance, and purity are the secret of true success. These principles, as set forth in the book of Proverbs, constitute a treasury of practical wisdom."[1] Yet and still, we've placed this treasure chest of wisdom on the shelf, picking it up for worship but never using it to figure out: how do I become a better leader? How can I add more value to my clients and customers?

Why don't we? The answer is simple. We have not allowed ourselves to explore how relevant the Scriptures are to our

---

1 . E. G. White, *Education*. Business Principles and Methods. (Mountain View, CA: Pacific Press Publishing Association, 1903), 135.1.

entrepreneurial endeavors. If we want our lives and our minds to be transformed, we need to change our lens.

The first element that we need to incorporate into our experience as Liberated Leaders is something I like to call Biblical Framing. Biblical Framing is a two-part process meant to make you more intentional about incorporating the Bible into your secular business. These two parts—application and interpretation—are how we direct our intentions.

Since our relationship to the Bible has to change, step one of Biblical Framing calls for us to look for the present-day application of the passages that we read. This doesn't mean that we neglect to appreciate the story or the spiritual lessons we glean from a passage. It simply means that we add an additional layer that has us asking questions like:

1. How would I feel if I were in this situation?
2. Have I seen something similar in my own life or in the life of someone else?
3. What principles are being shared in this passage that I can use today?

By asking these types of questions, we can look at the text in a way that makes it fresh.

Interpretation is the second phase of the process. This is where we allow what we've seen in the Scriptures to give us the proper context of our situation. While this may sound similar, there are some slight differences. Interpretation requires us to ask questions of the Scriptures to apply it to our situation. Application requires us to ask questions of our situations to apply Scripture.

Here's an example to clarify Biblical Framing further.

> *"And you shall remember that the Lord your God led you all the way these forty years in the wilderness, to humble you and test you, to know what was in your heart, whether you would keep His commandments or not. So He humbled you, allowed you to hunger, and fed you with manna*

which you did not know nor did your fathers know, that He might make you know that man shall not live by bread alone; but man lives by every word that proceeds from the mouth of the Lord." (Deuteronomy 8:2, 3 NKJV)

The first time I read these verses, I knew it was talking about the children of Israel, but I wanted to see how I could apply it to my life and my business. As I looked at all the heroes of the Bible, I noticed a pattern. No one ever got promoted without going through some type of wilderness. Abraham waited twenty-five years before the birth of his son. Joseph was in the prison for years before he was in the palace. Moses fed sheep for forty years before he started his mission. Daniel was a slave before he became a diplomat. In story after story, those who God called had a waiting period, and it was in the waiting where God was able to show them who they were and who He was. That got me thinking. If all these people had a period of waiting or wilderness before their breakthrough, then I should expect that God will test me and groom me in private before He will exalt me in public. This is the interpretation step.

One of the earliest challenges I had in business was being patient. I would always get frustrated that things wouldn't move as quickly as I wanted them to. I had a great idea, and I wanted it to take off right away. I didn't want to go through the process. I wanted what I wanted when I wanted it. I began to ask God about why He wasn't giving me the promotion. Eventually, I came to understand that God was not withholding from me what was good; He was simply giving me the time and space so I could be prepared to receive it. I was in the wilderness because I was being prepared for Canaan. This is application. The same verses were used from a different angle.

I know this was a simple example, but I can't tell you how many times I have had conversations with other entrepre-

neurs who don't see this. I don't blame them either. There are countless examples of those who stand in direct opposition to God's kingdom and are successful. In Psalm 73, David expressed the same sentiment when he said: "Behold, these are the ungodly,
/ Who are always at ease; / They increase in riches" (Psalm 73:12 NKJV). There are avenues to wealth that the unconverted heart pursues but that aren't available to the believer. They can lie, cheat, steal, and coerce, but verses 17 and 18 tell us that their end is destruction. Let me be clear and say that your faith is never a disadvantage. It is the greatest asset to your success if you allow God to work on your behalf.

When I was in college, I remember when Bernie Madoff was indicted and later sentenced to spend the rest of his life in prison because of the massive Ponzi scheme he created. For years, he seemed to be one of the darlings of the investing world. But as the Bible promises, Bernie's sins were found out and a decades-long career ended with public shame.

The amazing thing about God is that despite how things look, His desire is always to save us for time and eternity. That is why in our journey to have the mind of Christ, we need to cultivate our Biblical Framing skills. As we study God's Word, not only do we start to see the world the way God sees it, but we also begin to think the way He does.

There are countless examples of this method in Christ's ministry. Look at what happened during the Sermon on the Mount. For centuries, the Jews interpreted the law and the prophets through their human experience, not understanding God's intention. After coming out of His own wilderness experience, Christ's first public address begins to break down the misunderstandings and misconceptions within the people.

The people thought, like many do today, that it's not sin if you didn't do the deed. Jesus comes and reframes sin to be a result of a heart condition, not a hand condition. There was a spirit of legalism and pride that was pervasive. The

Savior challenged the "righteousness of the people" and showed them that none was worthy to cast judgment on their neighbor.

Point by point, Christ began to overturn all the false beliefs that had taken the minds of the people captive. Because He could see clearly, He could lead others out of darkness. This was Biblical Framing at its finest. Jesus—the Word made flesh and the world's Creator—is in conversation with man showing him how the world actually is.

What an advantage for us as Christian business owners. We have the privilege of seeing clearly by immersing ourselves in the Scripture. If we try to look at our lives and at our businesses without the lens of Scripture, we will fumble. I, as a glasses wearer, can think of times when I have put my glasses in a different place than where I normally put them. I wake up in the morning and reach on the nightstand, trying to find them. "Where are they?" I ask. I start to get a little uncomfortable because, without them, I can't see. My life comes to a standstill until I find what I know I need to see. Our day-to-day circumstances are the same. They require us to see clearly so we can make the best decisions possible, but day after day we settle for less than 20/20 vision. Why do we continue to move through life doing the same thing? We are struggling, reaching out, looking for vision, looking for clarity of purpose, but putting on everything but the glasses that we need to see clearly.

Without Biblical Framing, we struggle to make our customers the priority. We don't understand what it means to care for our employees. We don't know how to find the needs that need to be met in the marketplace. We can follow what the world says and have success. That may work for you, but I know that I want more than worldly success. I want to meet the heart needs of the people I'm called to serve. I want to introduce them to a Risen Savior. I want to be a conduit of love, joy, and blessing to those who need it most. That type of change requires more than what the world has to offer.

Conventional business wisdom tells us that we should constantly be reading and learning to develop ourselves as entrepreneurs. As a result of the challenges I faced with the restaurant, I decided to educate myself on how to be successful. The problem, though, was that as I read the books and listened to the podcasts, I began to focus on profits and wealth. Honoring God through my business became secondary. My worldly ambitions caused me to miss opportunities to serve my clients to the best of my ability. It made me nervous to share my faith with people who didn't believe like me. I saw seeds of greed and pride beginning to take root in my spirit. Praise God that I saw the change and corrected it!

I thought about Jeremiah 17:5-6 (NKJV), which says; "Thus says the Lord: / Cursed is the man who trusts in man / And makes flesh his strength, / Whose heart departs from the Lord. / For he shall be like a shrub in the desert, / And shall not see when good comes, / But shall inhabit the parched places in the wilderness, / In a salt land which is not inhabited." I saw that my business wasn't as fruitful for the kingdom as it could be. I was trusting the wisdom of other people more than the Creator of the world. Imagine the lifetime of missed opportunities for spreading the gospel that would have amassed if I didn't make the effort to seek God's wisdom first before the wisdom of men.

God is calling us to do through our businesses, and that's why it's so important to start with Biblical Framing.

Are you willing to make this shift?

If you are, I need you to do something before we move on. Put your right hand in the air and repeat after me.

I, _______ (that's where you put your name), solemnly swear that from here on out, I will be open to what the Scriptures have to say about me, about my business, and ultimately about the purpose of everything that I do as a Christian.

I acknowledge that some of these things may hurt. I acknowledge that some of these things may require sacrifice. But I know without a shadow of a doubt that I would rather be uncomfortable standing on truth than comfortable standing on a lie.

Give yourself a round of applause! Master this and you are one step closer to becoming that Liberated Leader, one step closer to thinking about your business the way Jesus would.

May 1, 2019

One of the reasons why I'm so optimistic that all of this will work out is because of my background. Not that I have to tell you, but for the sake of the record, I'll say that I'm an accountant.

I'm good at what I do, and I know that it will be a tremendous asset to the team. I've started running the numbers, and I know how much we need to make a month in order to stay afloat. I think $5,000 is the sweet spot, and based on how they said they're going to market the place, I think we should be good.

Dad is confident with what he knows about the area that it should work. I honestly don't know much, but I'm trusting their judgment.

As long as the numbers work, I'm good.

-L

August 17, 2019

The past few months have been a whirlwind. After much persuasion from my dad and the landlords, we opened July 4th. I wasn't particularly thrilled about that because I felt like we still needed more time to get ourselves together, but imperfect action, right?

Well, we had a couple large parties that came through and helped fill the tills with sales, but that seems to be short-lived. Outside of the events, people don't come through much. I'm starting to get a little worried about whether we'll be able to hit our revenue goals.

I'm still confident we can turn things around; we just need to get people in the doors. I'll try and get some coupons made up and run a couple ads. If we do that a couple times, I think it'll be sufficient to get some people in.

Still hoping for the best.

-L

Element #2: Self-Discovery

From the ages of zero to six, children are in a perpetual state of discovery. They're learning about the world around them, their bodies, language, and more. As the child grows, they continue to learn more about themselves and start to develop beliefs about who they are and what they are capable of. This process of self-discovery, at some point, should conclude with the now adult having a clear understanding of their personal purpose, strengths, weaknesses, and identity.

However, in today's technology-driven and privacy-averse society, it is becoming significantly harder for adults and youth alike to gain that type of clarity. That is why the second step in our Christ Mind Method is Self-Discovery. Part of what made Jesus so effective was His clear understanding of His identity and His purpose. The Gospel of Luke retells the story of young Jesus being left behind in Jerusalem after the Passover feast. When His parents finally realized He was missing (let's not talk about all the times we run ahead of Jesus in business, and it's days before we realize He's nowhere in sight), they returned to look for Him and found Him in the synagogue chatting with the scholars.

His mother, as I'm sure any mother would do, asked young Jesus why He would scare her like that. His response was profound.

And He said to them, "Why did you seek Me? Did you not know that I must be about My Father's business?" (Luke 2:49 NKJV)

This is the fruit of Self-Discovery. Jesus knew who He was. He knew why He had been born. He knew who had called Him. Jesus was so clear on everything that He came to the family business of salvation with a focus that many entrepreneurs are in need of.

Clarity is what allows you to articulate how you can help others. It makes it easier to enroll partners and employees. It helps direct your marketing efforts. It is everything you need in order to execute with intention and focus. Think about it: Jesus was asking the disciples to leave their homes, vocations, communities, friends, and family to follow Him. That level of ask requires a high level of clarity.

Might I say that many entrepreneurs then are struggling not from lack of passion or effort, but because they are out of alignment with who they are and what they are called to do?

I know this was my challenge. Part of why I was that Sinking CEO when I started my restaurant business was because I had a complete lack of self-awareness. I assumed that because I was good at one piece of the business, I was good at all aspects of it. I lacked clarity about my purpose. I was oblivious to my weaknesses. I was unprepared to receive instruction to help me improve, and it cost me my business.

As a result of the business failing, I began to take a hard look at myself. It was through the process of self-discovery that I uncovered my insecurities. I put a lot of pressure on myself to succeed. That led to me missing opportunities to make things better when I encountered challenges. I got real with myself about the areas of business I didn't know, like marketing and team management. I became aware of my perfectionist tendencies that led to periods of depression and shame when I made mistakes. When I finally became clear on all my stuff, I was able to make positive changes in my mindset that have improved my business acumen and helped me to find significant joy in the hills and valleys of entrepreneurship.

Self-Discovery is a crucial element in understanding our mindset. We know that Biblical Framing gives us a lens to interpret our circumstances. However, Self-Discovery helps us to see what is there to begin with and what needs to be changed.

Society will have us believe that we are great the way we are, that we have no flaws, and the incongruities in our character should be accepted and not changed. This is a fatal mistake. We are called as believers to a higher standard. Therefore, we need to be clear on who we are and how we think.

The first step in Self-Discovery is to **be aware of our reactions internally and externally.**

James 1:2-4 says: "My brethren, count it all joy when ye fall into divers temptations; Knowing this, that the trying of your faith worketh patience. But let patience have her perfect work, that ye may be perfect and entire, wanting nothing."

When we look at James 1 using the tools we acquired in Biblical Framing, we understand that the Bible is telling us that as we are tried or tested, we are perfected. What the text doesn't say—but it implies—is that perfection is a process. It starts with the test, and then as the broken parts of our lives come to the surface, we address the damage so we can grow into the fullness of who God created us to be.

As we mature and conquer a new challenge, the cycle continues. Testing, correcting, perfecting.

That is why every roadblock in business is necessary for our development. It is God's ordained method to help us gain a true knowledge of who we are. It exposes the areas for growth that we have, whether they include our ability to sell, to market, to assess a product, to be agile, to move quickly, or other areas. Even more, as a believer, it exposes the contents of our hearts.

I wish someone had told me this when I was struggling to make my business work. My inabilities to bring in customers, to properly manage a team, and to think and react quickly were being exposed. My lack of faith, harboring negative thoughts and emotions, and inappropriate reactions exposed my heart toward God.

This brings us to step two. Once we become aware of our reactions, we have to go back to God's Word to see if our reactions and attitude align with His mind.

When I was overwhelmed with anxiety and holding onto those thoughts that were so destructive, I was not allowing God to direct my steps. I was not keeping my mind fixed on Him. I was not prospering and in good health. I was outside of God's perfect will for my life and my business. I had allowed my circumstances to define me and was overcome.

When we look at Jesus, He was never overcome. He was tempted by Satan himself at His weakest points and still never allowed circumstance to define Him or distract from the mission. In the wilderness, every temptation was met with Scripture. Jesus had hidden the Word in His heart and refused to sin against God. The crisis came, and Christ's character was revealed.

I praise God that we still have hope. We still have time to correct the cracks in our character. Everything God does is bigger than we can imagine. It's bigger than your business. It's beyond you overcoming limiting beliefs and a millionaire mindset.

For the Christian, this is so much more than creating temporal success or building a legacy. Yes, a righteous man leaves an inheritance to his children's children, but the Bible was very clear to call him righteous. Our purpose in every area of life as a believer is to recommend the gospel to the people we serve—sometimes overtly, sometimes covertly, but never not at all. Our choices today impact us in this life and the life to come. This is the stuff that our eternal destiny depends on.

So when we search our heart, not by ourselves, but looking through Scripture, what do we actually find?

I didn't realize the extent of my brokenness until I was exposed. Business challenges, temptations, and trials can also expose our selfishness. No, we're not naturally inclined to choose holiness. We're not naturally inclined to choose faithfulness. We want what we want and never what the other person wants. Sin and death have wreaked havoc upon humanity.

Sin has transformed us from priests and kings to paupers. It's kept us from being Liberated Leaders and bound us to the fate of the Sinking CEO. It has stifled our God-given potential. As we look closer at the defects and the bruises and the scars that we have sustained in this thing called life, we become acutely aware of and can testify to what Scripture says when it tells us that we were formed in sin and shaped in iniquity (see Psalm 51:5).

Some of the things that I have seen about myself, and I'm sure you can relate, are quite surprising. There are decisions I've made and actions I've taken that I never thought I was capable of. It's not until character is revealed that you know the depths of how sin has influenced how you operate. So as we look closer, using Scripture as our guide and foundation to interpret our actions as good or evil, we become acutely aware of how desperately we need a renewal of our minds. We start to crave a new way of thinking. The greater the need, the greater the value. Once that's understood, we see how the mind of Christ has the potential to change everything.

This is a crucial step before we can work to correct it. If we were to compare this to an illness, the results of Self-Discovery would be the symptoms. The next thing to do would be to ascertain the cause of the symptoms, which we will do in the next chapter. Only then are we ready to apply the antidote.

October 16, 2019

Things are getting rough. The restaurant hasn't picked up at ALL. We've tried to get more customers, but we can't seem to get the numbers we need. Before we signed the lease, we were told that the owners of the space would be working to actively promote it. All we've seen is them trying to get more money.

It feels like we're completely alone. I'm starting to feel a little discouraged because we can't even make enough money to pay the team.

Maybe we should focus on being in the community. I'm not sure, but the tighter things get financially, the harder it is to think clearly.

I need something to change.

-L

November 13, 2019

This whole thing was a mistake. Seriously. Everything is crumbling around me. I found out a few weeks ago that I'm basically being let go from my job. How am I going to keep things afloat with no job?

I'm angry too. Every single week, I'm traveling across state lines to work. Trying to do a good job. Trying to keep up with this struggling business. And what did it get me? The exit.

Anyway, we're getting ready for Thanksgiving with some catering options. The menu is awesome, and I should be more excited. It's just like who's going to come anyway? We've had month after month of no income, and every week I get a call from someone who says we owe them money. Did I mention our rent goes up this month?

I wish I was more invested. Still motivated. Still optimistic. I try to be, but I'm tired. I'm starting to hate when people ask me about the business. I'd rather talk about the weather or politics. Really anything besides this. Maybe if I don't talk about it, no one will think differently about me.

I wish I could talk to someone about all this. The thing is, though, to admit I'm struggling: what does that mean for me? This is so embarrassing.

Let me go work on updating this site.

-L

Element #3: The Anatomy of Thought

Thoughts are funny things. When they are light and optimistic, we tend to question them. Yet when dark and discouraging thoughts come, we don't view them as anything other than true.

The subject of thought is something that seems to baffle the scientific community. Everything from the origin of thought to the purpose of why we as humans think comes with completely different opinions. Regardless of the disagreements, what psychologists and scientists all agree upon is that wherever or however thoughts come about, they are extremely powerful. They have the power to impact our actions, our emotions, our feelings, our performance, our relationships, and ultimately, our overall success in life and business.

Proverbs 23:7 tells us, "As he thinketh in his heart, so is he." Christ, echoing the sentiment, says during the Sermon on the Mount that if a man just looks at a woman and lusts after her, he's committed adultery in his heart (see Matthew 5:27-28). He adds that if you hate someone, you've committed murder in your heart (v. 21-22). Ultimately, Scripture is telling us that our thoughts are the foundation of our behavior, which at some point becomes habits, which then will lead to character.

Knowing this, we have to understand and appreciate that God invites us to get a thought tune-up.

Before we get to that, there's an important question to consider. "Where do thoughts even come from?" First Corinthians 4:7 tells us that everything we have we've received. If we use that as a basis to understand where thoughts come from, that means all thoughts have a source.

Let's look at a time when our thoughts were pure: at creation. In Genesis 2, we're introduced to Adam by name. He is perfect and made in the image of God, and he's been given an assignment. He's to name the animals, but he's not to name them because God is not sure what they're called. Scripture tells us that it was a test, that God wanted to see if the thoughts that Adam had were in line with God's thought. In verse 19, Adam joyfully begins his work. Each name that he gives the animals is exactly what they were called. They—Adam and God—were perfectly synced. Man thought like God, and there was no deviation.

Then sin comes in. The same serpent who in Revelation 12 drew a third of the stars (or angels) with his tail, shows up in the garden. The tail is mentioned for more than just imagery too. Isaiah 9:15 (NKJV) tells us, "The prophet who teaches lies, he is the tail." Therefore when the serpent, Satan, comes into the garden, he brings all his deceptions with him. He comes to this newly created race and attempts to gain their allegiance, to turn them against the Creator of the universe using the same methods he used in heaven: lies.

It was through these lies or words that Satan begins to plant thoughts in Eve's mind. Those thoughts then turn into a desire. Genesis 3:6 tells us that after the serpent tells Eve that she would not surely die if she ate the fruit, suddenly, her eyes are opened. It is as if she is seeing the fruit for the very first time, and what was previously off limits becomes extremely attractive. The thoughts that he planted—You won't die, you'll become a better version of yourself, God is trying to hold back something from you— became more believable than the thoughts God had given the first family. As a result of these new thoughts, the appearance of the fruit created the desire, that desire turned into action, and in one verse, we transition from paradise to a living hell. This is ground zero of the battle to control the minds of humanity.

Since his triumph in Eden, Satan has desired to put his thoughts in our minds. Similarly, God, since the fall of humanity, has been trying to get us perfectly synced again. He never wanted the connection to be broken. He didn't want us to be confused about His plans or not desiring to know the thoughts that He has for us. He wanted us to think like Him, so we could enjoy Him, so we could learn and grow and reach the highest possible heights as His crowning jewel of creation. Continuing through the Genesis account, we get to Genesis 3:15, which gives us the promise that this serpent—the one that has caused so much pain and suffering—will be destroyed, but he wasn't going down without a fight. Skip over a few chapters, and we get to Genesis 6.

If you do not remember, this is the account of the flood. The Bible tells us that the thoughts of the people were evil continually. They thought like Satan. They did the works of Satan. They were corrupt in their hearts and minds like Satan. So when Satan sees this, he begins to think that he's won. Except there is a family. A family that thinks like God, and Noah, receiving the impressions on his mind from the word of God, begins to build an ark.

By faith Noah, being warned of God of things not seen as yet, moved with fear, prepared an ark to the saving of his house; by the which he condemned the world, and became heir of the righteousness which is by faith. (Hebrews 11:7)

Satan doesn't succeed, but he keeps trying. From Abraham, Isaac, and Jacob to the children of Israel making a golden calf in the wilderness, the struggle rages on. From glory to apostasy, the cycle continues. From the judges, the kings, and the prophets to being exiled in Babylon, God continues to pursue the creations that Satan tries to destroy, and it is all through the minds of humanity.

God puts thoughts in Nebuchadnezzar's mind while he sleeps and gives him a dream that outlines the course of human history up until the return of Jesus Christ. Jeremiah, a bold preacher for truth, receives the word or thoughts of God and speaks only the things that God directs. Story after story, we see the forces of light and darkness trying to impress thoughts into the minds of the people.

Then the promised Messiah comes. In Christ, we see what is possible when our minds are, once again, reconnected with God's. Christ's mind is fortified. It is fortified through prayer and the Scriptures. Though He knows that the enemy will attack Him and things will become inexpressibly hard, Jesus never gives an opportunity for Satan to control Him by the avenue of His thoughts. As He is tempted in the wilderness, He meets the challenge with a "thus saith the Lord." It was because of this that He can say in John 14:30, "The prince of this world cometh, and hath nothing in me." How incredible is that? Whatever His Father told Him to say, whatever His Father told Him to do, whatever thought was placed in His mind by the Father were the ones that He was actuated by and never anything else. This is the same experience that the gospel makes available to us.

The sheep hear the voice of the Shepherd, and they know it, and they follow it. Are we abiding? Are we hearing? Are we listening? I remember years ago I had a little health scare. I didn't think there was anything wrong, but I had a thought in my mind that was impossible to shake. It kept telling me, "You're sick, you're sick, you're sick." I would be at work, I would be at church, I would be in my bed, and this thought would come, and it would pierce, and it would shut down everything else around me. I remember thinking and praying, "Lord, I do not believe this. I don't believe this, but I'm starting to feel fear because this thought keeps coming into my mind."

After months of the attacks, I went to the doctor. Praise God, I was right and there was nothing wrong. My faith in God proved to be the answer. Everything was clear, and immediately the thoughts stopped. It was from that moment on that I realized how powerful the warfare is around us. We have thoughts constantly being impressed upon our minds. We have to understand that thoughts are the results of an input, similar to how we can type a sentence on a keyboard and it will show up on our screen. The words didn't just happen magically, but the input that we put in by our fingers hitting the keys now leads to the output that we see on the screen. Our thoughts are the same way. But sometimes as Christians, we think so much in the physical that it becomes hard for us to discern the spiritual. That is why Paul writes in Ephesians 6 that our warfare isn't against flesh and blood, it's spiritual, and so we have to stop fighting a spiritual battle with carnal means.

I'm sure you're probably thinking, "What does all of this have to do with running a business?" It's simple. Ministry requires money. Every school, hospital, church, Bible, missionary, and minister requires funds to be put in place. Therefore, it is to Satan's advantage to keep God's people from obtaining the resources they need to fund ministry.

Take John as an example.

John is a mechanic. He's good at what he does and loves serving in his local church. John has a brother, Eric, who served some time and found Christ while incarcerated, but he found it hard to find a job after his release. Because of the changes he saw in Eric, John's dream is to work with ex-offenders helping them get them reintroduced to society by learning a trade and showing them the peace and joy one can have in Christ. He'd love to turn his mechanic shop into a ministry hub, but he is discouraged by how things have been going financially. He's been struggling to pay the guys that he has now and has concluded the program would be nearly impossible to pull off. He begins to think that he doesn't deserve to be successful and that maybe he should settle for being able to feed his family. He returns his tithe weekly but doesn't have enough money to give to the different missions. He wishes he had more to give and feels bad even thinking about more money.

If John wants to make the impact he desires for his family and the community, he will need to overrule the thoughts of lack and failure that Satan has planted in his mind. This is where the R.E.W.I.R.E. toolkit that we'll discuss in the next chapter comes in. By rewiring how he thinks, John can create a new reality for himself. He can be confident knowing that God wants him to succeed. He can begin to change how he charges for his services. He can find ways to bring more income into the shop without having to be the one doing the work. By operating in harmony with what God really thinks, John can finally be free to make a difference for today and for eternity.

Satan's number one objective is to cripple the work of the gospel. Part of his plan is to keep believers like John in a state of lack, despite all the biblical promises that point to abundance, prosperity, and success when we are surrendered to God.

Satan knows that, in the hand of the Liberated Leader, money becomes food for the hungry, education and shelter for the orphan, treatment for the sick, community for the lonely, and employment for the poor. It can change the world and fulfill the promise of the gospel being preached to all the nations and then the end of the world coming (see Matthew 24:14). It is in Satan's best interest that we get stuck in the quagmire of limiting beliefs. Like:

- "I don't know if anybody wants the service I have."
- "I don't know if I can be a Christian in the marketplace."
- "I will never be successful."
- "I don't know if I'm able to learn this."
- "I can never have a six- or seven- or eight-figure business."
- "God doesn't want me to be wealthy because wealthy people are evil."
- "If I get money, I'm going to be greedy."
- "If I get money, I won't know how to use it."

These and many other thoughts are the reasons why we don't have as much power as we could.

What we need instead is victory. Victory isn't just for you or your family. This is so much bigger than you. This is playing an integral part in finishing the work of preaching the gospel that can save a sin-sick world and prepare people to meet their God.

This is so much deeper than awards or funnels or client acquisition or sales calls. This is about being able to make an impact for eternity. I started this section talking about where thoughts come from with the garden and Genesis, but I want to just quickly go to the end of the book, Revelation. And in Revelation 14, John describes a group of people referred to as 144,000, and those people are redeemed from the earth; they're spotless and perfect before God.

What does that mean? When this is all said and done, there will be a people, a group of people, 144,000 people, who are perfectly synced with the mind of Christ. The R.E.W.I.R.E. Toolkit is the final element we need to become the Liberated Leader God wants us to be.

December 20, 2020

Hello old friend. A lot has changed since we last spoke. The pandemic came and forced us to close our doors. I can't say that I was disappointed. Besides, it gave my ego an out. We went on to tie up loose ends, and instead of looking for a new location, we put all the equipment, along with the memories, into a storage unit. Only to revisit it in our thoughts.

I've done a lot of growing since then. I realize how much I allowed my own thoughts and insecurities to shape the challenges I was facing.

There were real pressures. No one can take that from me. Nevertheless, what you focus your attention on gets your intention. I don't think I understood how much I was unraveling what I wanted for so long because I wasn't willing to shift.

I still want to have my own business. I'm thinking about starting something new next year. I've got a little more grit than I did before. Maybe this was all worth it. Time will tell.

-L

The Final Element: REWIRE Toolkit

The final step in the Christ Mind method is the REWIRE Toolkit. The strategies that I'm about to go over are the same ones that defined the gospel business of Christ and are exactly what we need to finally become the Liberated Leader we were created to be.

God wants us to think like Him. He is looking for a generation of Liberated Leaders who will shine the light of Heaven into a dark world. He wants us to share the Good News of a Risen Savior and the power to be changed into a character fit for the presence of the Omnipotent.

We were, in the beginning, made in the image of God. All of heaven is uniting to restore man back to where he fell from. At the start, we thought like God and did the works of God. In Jesus, we have the power to do so again. If we want to think like Jesus, we need to do what Jesus did so we can have the same mindset and the same success that He obtained.

I'm sure you've heard that success leaves clues. All through the Bible, we get more and more information so we can discern our true identity. Nevertheless, there is one place that requires further investigation—the sanctuary.

A lot of believers know about the Old Testament sanctuary that Moses pitched, but they kind of leave it in the Old Testament saying, "That covenant was fulfilled on the cross." But there's something very, very important for us to remember: everything in the sanctuary is a type or a symbol of what God's kingdom is like. We get some insight on that point in the Book of Hebrews. But for those of you who don't really remember what the Old Testament sanctuary looked like, let me give you a quick refresher. You can find this all in Exodus, starting in chapter 25 through the end of the book. Leviticus also gives some additional information about the sanctuary services.

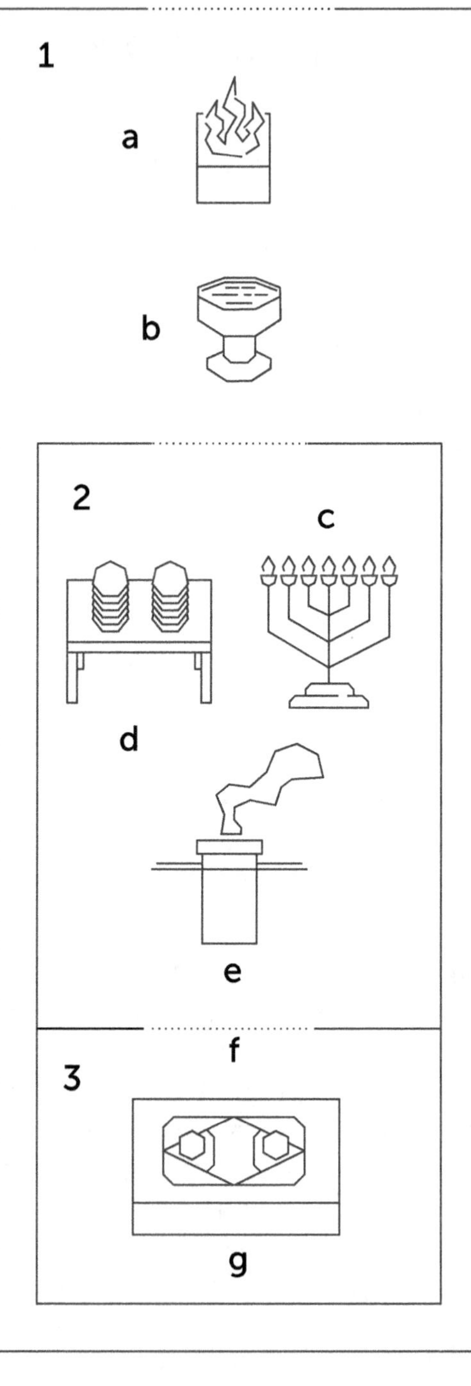

1
a
b
2
c
d
e
f
3
g

The sanctuary was set up in three parts: the outer court (1), the Holy Place (2), and the Most Holy Place (3). The boundaries of the sanctuary were marked, and they separated the congregation (the children of Israel) from the wherever the sanctuary was pitched. The boundaries created the outer court. When you entered the outer court, you came first to the altar of sacrifice (a), then the laver (b). In the center of the court, there was a semi-permanent structure that was divided by a veil into two separate compartments: the Holy Place (2) and the Most Holy Place (3). When you entered the structure—the sanctuary—you went into the first compartment and found the seven-branch candlestick (c), the table of shewbread (d), and the altar of incense (e). Then moving beyond the veil (f), you came into the Most Holy Place (3), and that is where you found the presence of God—the shekinah glory—resting on the mercy seat that was set on top of the ark of the covenant (g). Each piece was specifically designed to tell a part of the redemption story.

Now that you have that background, let's talk about why this is important. In Psalm 77:13, we learn that God's way or plan for everything can be found in the sanctuary. Therefore, this is where we must look for our antidote. When we look at the Holy Place, we find the tools that make us fit to be in God's presence and the basis for the R.E.W.I.R.E. Toolkit.

The altar of incense represents prayer (see Revelation 8:3), the table of shewbread represents the Word of God (see Matthew 4:4), and the seven-branch candlestick represents witnessing (see Matthew 5:14-16).

Before we can implement the R.E.W.I.R.E. Toolkit, we must be actuated by the Spirit. Therefore, prayer is the first component. Ask God to give you victory over toxic thoughts. Pray for wisdom on how to run your business in a way that glorifies Him. Pray that He will show you the truth about yourself. All these important prayers are answered through the moving of the Spirit.

From there, we prayerfully open our toolkit.
R.E.W.I.R.E. stands for:

R – Recognize
E – Examine
W – Wastebasket
I – Integrate
R – Reinforce
E – Educate Others

RECOGNIZE

The first step in having our minds transformed is to recognize when thoughts come to our mind that impact our lives and our businesses.

We have gotten so accustomed to just having these inputs come into our mind that we never challenge them. But remember I told you the story about my health crisis and how I refused to claim that thought as truth. You must recognize when those thoughts come in. As I mentioned earlier, one of the thoughts I recognized was that I was attaching my self-worth to my business's success or failure.

EXAMINE

Once you recognize the thoughts—that's acknowledging the thoughts—then you need to examine the nature or the fruit of the thoughts. Are they good fruits? Are they of a pure nature? Or are they rotten fruits and of a vile nature? Examine them; understand who is placing them in your mind.

Going back to my self-worth being linked so closely to my business, I really had to examine not only why I felt that but also how it was impacting me. It was this examination that helped me see that I was preventing myself from seeing opportunities all around me.

WASTEBASKET

After we recognize the thoughts that impact our life and business and we examine the thoughts to know the nature and the fruit of those thoughts, we wastebasket, which means we discard the impure, inaccurate, and damaging thoughts. I must warn you, though, that this is going to be a foreign concept. It is not going to feel natural for you to reject thoughts. It requires you to, when a damaging thought comes to your mind, choose to not accept it. No longer will you be a passive thinker accepting everything that comes your way as truth. You will begin to guard your mind and select the things that you will and will not believe. Over time, you'll find that those thoughts no longer come, and as you continue to do the exercise, it will strengthen like a muscle.

I know that for me, it was a struggle to overcome my self-worth issues. It required me to get real about my relationship to money, past financial traumas, and the status of my faith. I had to acknowledge and reject thoughts of unworthiness and integrate new thoughts from God's Word, which is the next step.

INTEGRATE

Integrate new Word-inspired thoughts into your life. Jesus's story about the man with devils (see Luke 12:24-26) tells us how a devil was cast out from a man, but the man didn't fill the house back up. So, what happened? The devil returned, and he brought with him seven other spirits that were even more wicked than him. We can't just wastebasket the thoughts that aren't serving us; we must replace them. Write down the thoughts that you have identified as harmful and why. Then take some time to find Bible passages that counteract those thoughts. If you struggle with being materialistic, find verses that talk about humility. If you struggle to speak kindly to your team, find a text that talks about how the righteous communicate.

Our strength is in the power of God's Word to transform our hearts and minds. So it's only right that as we remove these negative thoughts, we replace them with the fruit of God's Word.

REINFORCE

The next step is to reinforce the newly cultivated thoughts through prayer, meditation on the Word, and memorization. If memorization is something that you struggle with, I invite you to visit the website where you can find memory verse cards to help you integrate more of God's Word into your everyday life. To learn more, visit: www.letthismindbook.com/memorycards.

EDUCATE OTHERS

It's commonly said that if you know something really well, you can teach it. Therefore, you need to educate others about what you have learned. What is the purpose of recognizing your thoughts, examining your thoughts, throwing away the thoughts that are not in line with God's Word or God's plan for your life, integrating new thoughts, and reinforcing them through prayer and meditation on His Word if you don't share it?

By teaching what you've discovered, you also reinforce what you know because you're using the information in a different way. Why do you think I wrote a book? Not only do I want to help you, but I also want to make sure I never forget the things God has shown me through entrepreneurship.

You don't have to wait to share either! You can share your insights with your prayer group. You can share them with your employees, your mentors, or your mentees. I also want to encourage you to share them on the Let This Mind Facebook page, or you can join the Let This Mind community where we talk about these types of things in a safe space, and that can be found on the website.

When implemented, these six simple elements will have a profound impact on your life. What I love so much about the REWIRE Toolkit is the simplicity. It's not overwhelming. It's not too hard for you to do, and the Spirit is waiting with open arms to help you. As you seek to have the mind of Christ, commune with Him, read His Word, and see how Christ thought—and as you behold Him—you will become changed.

The Bigger Picture

"Let this mind be in you, which was also in Christ Jesus."
Philippians 2:5

At this point, we've gone through all the steps. We've talked about how Biblical Framing is imperative to how we view our circumstances. We reviewed the elements of Self-Discovery and the Anatomy of Thought. We made it all practical with the R.E.W.I.R.E. Toolkit. So that's it, right? Not quite. You see, if I were to let you ride off into the sunset with the information you've received to this point, you'd leave with just that: information. My whole goal with this book has been to give you a transformation, a shift in perspective and in your Christian experience.

When Paul told the Philippian church to have the mind of Christ, he revealed to them the key that would unlock all the riches of heaven for then and for eternity. It is only by thinking the way Christ thought that they could understand the power that was available to them and the work that could be accomplished through them. It would be the catalyst for unity amongst the body. It would bear witness of the gospel to the unconverted. It would bring the church true success. Through a renewed mind, the Philippians would be restored to the image of God.

Praise God that the same invitation is made to us two thousand years later. We can become a generation of believers whose minds are so in harmony with the mind of Christ that our influence is inevitable.

I want it to be clear that while the Christ Mind Method can transform how you do business from a practical standpoint, it is also the key to creating substantial impact on behalf of the kingdom of God. When we allow our motives to be dictated by the Word of God, we become the greatest ambassadors for the gospel in the marketplace. We can reach those who are seemingly unreachable to the clergy. We can become beacons of light and hope in our communities that are open way more often than for a few hours on the weekend. We become driven by the love of Christ to do more for all those who we encounter.

This is the fruit of having the mind of Christ. It is to esteem the well-being, future health, prosperity, and happiness of others more than your own. It's a call to become self-sacrificing in a world that is becoming more and more self-serving by the day. Christ walked the earth for thirty-three years consistently seeking to serve those around Him. It was never fake, never with ulterior motives or feigned interest. It was real and grounded in genuine love for people and for His Father.

As Liberated Leaders, we are called to do more than make money, though making money is not a bad thing. It allows us the opportunity to be benefactors for the cause of Christ. However, we are called to utilize every gift and talent to glorify God. We strive for excellence because we serve an excellent God. We show love to our employees, customers, and other business partners because God is love. We maintain the highest level of integrity because our God keeps His word. We are called to make Christ relevant in the marketplace. Every sale, coaching call, tax return, alteration, paint job, logo, piece of copy, contract, or conversation is an opportunity to demonstrate the love of God in a meaningful way. And as we seek to uplift the kingdom, we have the promise that everything that we need will be provided (see Matthew 6:33).

The principles laid out in this book are just the beginning. I hope that you're beginning to understand that we can have the mind of Christ even in business. Not only was Christ strategic, but He was also our perfect example. We need not look to other people who are just as flawed, troubled, challenged, unsure, and insecure as we are. We have a better example. When we seek to be transformed by the renewing of our minds, we are empowered to think, strategize, communicate, rally, and build a movement the same way Christ did. And we are also called to live a life of holiness and righteousness in a similar fashion.

I cannot wait until I get to see a generation of Liberated

Leaders who are endowed with the mind of Christ, and I can observe the impact they have on the world. Our teams would be stronger spiritually, mentally, and emotionally. There would be a marked difference in the level of service that customers and clients receive. Marketing efforts would be based on a deeper desire to serve and not simply profits. Nothing would be left undone or incomplete. If we would only surrender.

Entrepreneurship is hard, but nowhere near as hard as the plan of redemption. I would argue that the mindset that Christ had during His earthly ministry can have a supernatural effect on our ability to perform in our businesses. It's time to make the Word practical.

The understanding of what has become available to us through faith in Jesus is the key to becoming Liberated Leaders. This is my story. My truth. Now it's time for you to write your own story. May God bless you richly. Amen.

August 1, 2021

It seems like every week I'm having a breakthrough. I've matured in my thinking. I'm embracing the hills and valleys of my experience. I'm no longer grasping for success but enjoying the process. I think that's what God wanted for me all along. It's so much easier to rest in God's will and His timing than to struggle against His providence.

I'm still working on building myself as an entrepreneur, but I have patience. I have endurance. I have a willingness to put up with whatever storms come my way because I know on the other side is everything that God has prepared for me.

This is all I've got for now. We'll talk again soon, friend.

All my love.

-L

Section 2:
The Gospel Business – Marketplace Case Studies

Marketplace Answers from the Gospel

The following case studies are some common problems I've seen entrepreneurs face in business. To address them, I have taken some examples from the ministry of Christ to help you start thinking about present-day challenges in business through the lens of the gospel. Remember, Jesus had a business. Therefore, we can glean a whole lot from how He addressed different challenges.

How to Launch a New Business and Build a Team without Lots of Time, Money, or an Existing Audience

One of the hardest things that new business owners struggle with is how to build an audience that is interested in what they offer. The second hardest thing is to find solid people to join your team.

How much easier would business be if you had an audience ready to hear what you have to say and people who immediately bought into your movement?

This is possible, and you don't need:

- A lot of money
- To come from a large town
- To have gone to the best schools

Prior to His baptism, Jesus was—by the world's standards—a nobody. Given the pervasive misunderstanding of the Messiah in those days, He was seemingly uninteresting. So much so that when Jesus returned to His hometown to teach and declared His true identity, they got angry and threw Him out of the town (see Luke 4:28, 29)

His parents weren't wealthy. He was born into a low-income, working-class family. He never had any formal education, but He had a calling and a time limit (see Daniel 9:25, 26).

To build His reputation quickly and start gaining momentum, He did the following:

Number 1: Jesus understood that He needed help and the type of people who would be a good fit.

From the beginning of time, the Godhead always operated in community, and as Christ began to understand His identity in childhood and live it out in adulthood, He continued to emphasize community. Christ knew that for Him to finish the work and to build a movement that would last after His work on earth was done, He needed to build a team that He could train. He also found support, friendship, love, and companionship in the team that He built. Jesus knew He needed a team and made it a priority.

Too many entrepreneurs are eager to be on their own, but they miss out on the diversity of ideas, skills, and talents found in community. Don't allow money to deter you. Leverage the relationships you already have to find people who are willing to buy in before the payout. One of the things that I've always done is to connect with my local church community to find the things I need. I have found service providers, opportunities for partnership, employees, and new connections all because of existing relationships. Get uncomfortable and ask the people in your network for what you need. You'll be surprised to learn that you have not because you ask not.

Number 2: He understood timing.

While Jesus was in the wilderness, John the Baptist was arrested. Because of his teaching, John grew a following and even had disciples. When Jesus came from His temptation, He started building His team and began with Andrew and Simon Peter, who knew of John's ministry and were now unoccupied after his arrest. Jesus did not pull them from an active ministry at its peak; He knew that the time was right.

When you're looking for people to build your team, don't take people from the good work that they're already doing. This is not to be misunderstood to mean that you cannot extend an opportunity to someone who already has a job or commitment. What I am saying is to get an understanding of their openness to something new. Have a conversation about what their current goals and responsibilities are. Ultimately, you need to understand the timing.

Number 3: He leveraged someone else's platform.

A lot of times when we look at the story of Jesus, we take for granted that John baptized Him. Yes, we know that it was ordained by God and was supposed to happen, but John was famous. He was an influencer in his day, and when Jesus came to be baptized on his platform, this was a big deal.

Ask yourself why John didn't baptize Jesus in private. Couldn't that have been sufficient? Not at all! When it was time for Jesus to start His ministry, He needed to be forced into the public eye. This was the perfect platform to launch His Father's business.

Are you leveraging the platforms of others in your space? One of the quickest ways for you to develop brand awareness and trust with your potential customers is to share space with the people they already know, like, and trust. In this social media age, there are countless platforms for you to take advantage of. You can be featured on someone's podcast. You can go live on Facebook or Instagram with an influencer. You can connect with a blogger or YouTuber to create an affiliate deal. You can join or present to relevant community organizations. Don't try to create a platform from scratch. Leverage the platforms that have already been built.

How to Overcome Sales Objections

Have you ever been in a situation where you have your ideal customer in front of you and they're interested in your product or service, but you couldn't seem to close the sale? How frustrating is it to be right at the finish line, but you can't convert?

What would happen to your business if you increased your closing rate by ten percent? Who would you be able to add to your team? How could you improve your marketing or product offerings? Would that be the difference between paying yourself well and taking the crumbs?

You can increase your sales conversion rate without:

- Coming off as greedy
- Making your customer feel like they were forced into a sale

Jesus was a master communicator. He understood that in any transaction, people do things for their own reasons and not His. Here's the Savior of the world coming with the investment opportunity of a lifetime, but He never pitched His product based on what it did for Him. He was always concerned about the well-being of the buyer and made sure that they made an empowered decision.

One of the best accounts in the Scriptures for overcoming objections is in John 4. There, Jesus converts a skeptical Samaritan woman into a disciple of the gospel in her city.

The steps that Jesus used demonstrate how even the simplest things can be viewed through a spiritual context. This conversation also gives the entrepreneur insight on how we turn skeptical spectators into raving fans.

Number 1: Jesus allowed the environment to determine the context of the conversation.

John 4:6 opens the scene with Jesus sitting on the edge of Jacob's well, tired from traveling, and it's about noon or the sixth hour of the day. If you've ever tried to do anything in the summer at midday, you know it's hot. There is this woman who comes to draw water. This is the context Christ leverages to start a conversation.

Whether you are approaching a potential customer or if a customer is coming to you, you must understand the context of the conversation. Was it the result of a speaking engagement? Did they find you on social media? Were they referred to you by someone else? All these elements matter because they help you create a selling experience that puts your customers at ease. By being aware of the circumstances, you are able to direct the conversation in the best way possible.

For example, if I'm giving a presentation on how you can increase the profits in your fitness business through marketing and you come up to me after that presentation wanting to schedule a meeting, it would make sense to frame the potential sales conversation around what marketing strategies have and have not worked for your fitness business. On the flipside, it would not make sense to get to the conversation and talk about cutting your labor costs in order to increase your profits. Knowing the context helps you determine the content.

Going back to the story, Jesus observes the time. He knows that it isn't normal for women to come in the heat of the day to draw water. Therefore, water was a great conversation starter.

Number 2: Jesus asked questions to get the woman to engage in conversation.

It was well-known that the Jews and Samaritans didn't get along. The Jews felt that they were better than the Samaritans, and the Samaritans hated the arrogance of the Jews. Knowing this, Jesus, operating from a place of sincerity, asks the woman for a drink of water. In a book called Desire of Ages, the author says: "In the East, water was called 'the gift of God.' To offer a drink to the thirsty traveler was held to be a duty so sacred that the Arabs of the desert would go out of their way in order to perform it."[2] This question was the key to opening the woman's heart to conversation.

When engaging in sales conversations, ask questions of your prospect. Seek to understand what is important to them and use this information to get them to open up to you. As they become more open, you build trust and position yourself as a friend and trusted advisor.

Number 3:Jesus demonstrated understanding of the woman's perceived need, while looking to meet her actual need.

Going back to the context, it was clear that this woman had something keeping her from drawing water early in the morning like the other women of the city. She was avoiding the crowd because of some unspoken shame. Understanding that the woman was looking to escape the pain she was in, Christ mentions the living water that He could provide for her (vv. 10-15).

Stop trying to sell people your thing for your reason. Your customer only wants to buy for their reasons. If you demonstrate a clear understanding of their need and how your solution meets their need, they will be much more likely to at least hear more.

Number 4: Jesus showed that He could meet her real need and delivered.

When it was time for Jesus to deliver on His promise, He did. In verse 25, the Samaritan woman finally sees that her greatest need is to be converted. The shame and longings of her heart would be met when she finally found the Messiah. Then in verse 26, Jesus tells her that He is who she's been waiting for. Immediately, she is sold. She then goes to tell everyone she can. Because of her, Jesus is able to spend two days in Samaria ministering to the people.

As entrepreneurs, we are called to solve the problems we see in the world. Don't just meet people's needs in word; you must deliver.

---

2 E. G. White, Desire of Ages, (Mountain View, CA: Pacific Press Publishing Association, 1898), 183.4

Three Keys to Become the Type of Leader That People Follow and Customers Gravitate To

Many entrepreneurs struggle to stand out from the crowd. They lack clarity on what makes them different from the rest. They do things in the same way that they've always been done.

It's time to step up as that Liberated Leader and leave uncertainty in the dust.

There were three keys that Jesus used in His ministry so that He could become someone who people gravitated to, helping Him accomplish more in a limited timeframe.

Key #1: Jesus was clear about His purpose and His product.

In John 17, we find one of Jesus's last prayers before the cross. In verse 4, He says that the work He was given to do was completed. Part of what made this possible was the fact that Jesus was clear on who He was and what He came to bring to the world. Lack of clarity leads to confusion, which leads to wasted time. Jesus never participated in discussions or activities that didn't further move Him toward accomplishing His goal.

Want to become the type of leader people follow? Make sure you maintain the highest level of clarity. You should be able to articulate what you do in a sentence. You should be able to tell how you can help quickly. Don't allow yourself to get distracted by all the things you could do.

Key #2: He wasn't looking to maintain the status quo.

One of the biggest hindrances to Christ's ministry was the scholars of the day. In everything He did, they were always looking for an opportunity to correct Jesus or tell Him that what He did violated their customs. Jesus was not interested in maintaining the status quo because that's what they always did.

He was moved by principle and made sure to offer the people a clear understanding of what their investment in the kingdom of God actually meant.

Don't be afraid to go against the grain. God has given each of us a measure of His creativity. We should look for new and innovative ways to reach the market with our products and services. Our goal as entrepreneurs isn't simply about making money. It's about making the lives of our communities better.

Key #3: Jesus was committed to delivering excellent service.

Excellent customer service means regardless of what we need to do, we make our customers feel our love. In Mark 6, Jesus spends the day teaching the multitudes and knows that they need to eat. Instead of sending the people away hungry, He asks the disciples to feed the people. In that desert place, Jesus spreads a table in the wilderness as He had done centuries before for the children of Israel. He demonstrated His care for the whole person.

Is excellent service one of your core values? When people patronize your business, do they feel that they've been cared for and not sold to? Look for opportunities to go above and beyond. It will not only create lifelong customers, but it will also be an opportunity to recommend the gospel.

The One Thing Every Leader Should Teach Their Team

Many entrepreneurs make the mistake of thinking that because they operate a certain way, the people that work with them will be the same way. We have to remember that we all view the world differently. Transformational leaders don't try to change the personality of their team, but they cultivate employees into the best version of themselves.

Therefore, the one thing every leader should teach their team is how to think.

Key #1: Jesus saw the potential in His disciples.

When we look at the disciples that Christ chose, we may ask, "Why of all people did He choose them? What did Christ see in them?"

Take Peter, for example. Peter was quick tempered and quick to assert himself. Jesus knew that Peter was a leader, although uncultivated. He wanted to work with Peter and refine him. John, who loved Him from the beginning, was the youngest disciple. He saw that caring nature, and He knew that through John, the love of Christ could be shared abroad. Matthew was a tax collector. Jesus understood that, although he had an issue with honesty, the precision and accuracy that Matthew had to be able to do his job as a tax collector would be invaluable to the ministry.

Always look at the potential of your team and equip them so that you can bring out the best in them. Pay close attention to the things that come naturally to them. Are they good communicators? Do they excel at organizing things? Are they extremely outgoing and personable? Whatever good you see, acknowledge it and see how it can be cultivated into a superpower.

One of the greatest things that happened to me in college was my accounting professor. Even though I had spent the first two years of my college experience goofing off, I had one professor take an interest in me and see my potential. It was because of him that I ended up being a teacher's assistant for the same class that I had almost failed. He saw that I had talent that needed to be cultivated and invested countless hours to give me the support I needed. I'm forever grateful to him. When you demonstrate belief in your team, it will encourage them to think about themselves at a higher level.

Key #2: He gave His disciples room to make mistakes.

We have to give our team room to make mistakes. I love the story of Christ in Mark 9:14-29. After He comes down from the Mount of Transfiguration, He finds the remaining disciples embarrassed because they were supposed to be casting out a devil from a young boy and they were unable to do it.

Seeing the issue, Jesus rebukes the demon, and the boy is restored to his father in his right mind. The crowd begins to chastise the disciples and asks why they couldn't do this. Discouraged, the disciples ask Jesus the same question privately. Instead of embarrassing them, He kindly answers that some of these things come only by prayer and fasting. Not once did Jesus make them feel bad. He took the opportunity to educate them and make them better.

In order for our teams to become better thinkers, we need to give them room to make mistakes. It is in making mistakes that the lesson is seared in the mind.

Key #3: Jesus led by example.

Whatever Christ asked His disciples to do, He was willing to do Himself. Before He went to the cross, Jesus washed the feet of all the disciples. Imagine this: the King of Glory washing the dust off the feet from whence man was drawn. Such a profound example of humility and grace. As He finishes, He says: "If I then, your Lord and Master, have washed your feet; ye also ought to wash one another's feet" (John 13:14).

As leaders, we should never be too good to do the lowliest tasks in our companies. As we demonstrate true leadership and what it means to think like Christ, we begin to instill the same practices in those who are under our governance.

Thinking is more than a thought appearing out of thin air. It is a continual yielding to God's leading so that we can do the best for all those in our sphere of influence.

What's Next?

I hope that this book has blessed you as much as it has been a blessing for me to write. If you would like to continue the conversation, I invite you to join the LTM community. In the community, you will find weekly teachings, study guides, and other resources designed to help you on your journey to becoming the entrepreneur that God has called you to be. To learn more, visit www.letthismindbook.com/community.

About the Author

Lawron Ballard is a speaker, author, and founder of The Discipling CPA, LLC— an accounting and business consultancy firm. Lawron is a graduate of Temple University in Philadelphia and began her career at Deloitte in 2011, where she worked with various multinational Fortune 100 companies. She is also the host of the Biblical Business podcast.

When she's not serving her clients, she's enjoying nature, watching a docuseries or snuggling up with a good book.

While accomplishments are great, Lawron's desire is to be known as a woman who is on a continual journey to understand what it means to live by every word that proceeds from the mouth of God.

www.ingramcontent.com/pod-product-compliance
Lightning Source LLC
LaVergne TN
LVHW020653100826
845148LV00012B/2458